Everything
You Need to
Know About

# Bipolar
# Disorder and
# Manic
# Depressive
# Illness

In the fifth century BC, Hippocrates treated people for "melancholia," which we now know as depression.

# Everything You Need to Know About Bipolar Disorder and Manic Depressive Illness

Michael A. Sommers

THE ROSEN PUBLISHING GROUP, INC.
NEW YORK

*To Jesse, who is not bipolar but who has dealt with a lot of depressed people.*

Published in 2000 by The Rosen Publishing Group, Inc.
29 East 21st Street, New York, NY 10010

First Edition

**Library of Congress Cataloging-in-Publication Data**

Sommers, Michael A., 1966-
 Everything you need to know about bipolar disorder and manic depressive illness / by Michael A. Sommers
     p.  cm.
 Includes bibliographical references and index.
 Summary: Defines bipolar disorder and manic-depressive illness, explains how they affect teenagers, and how they are treated.
 ISBN  0-8239-3106-4 (lib. bdg.)
     1. Manic-depressive illness—Juvenile literature. [1. Manic-depressive illness. 2. Mental illness.] I. Title.
RC516.S655 2000
616.89'5—dc21                                        99-042087
                                                          CIP
                                                          AC

*Manufactured in the United States of America*

# Contents

# Introduction

Depression has been around since the beginning of human history. In biblical times, Saul, who became the first king of Israel, suffered from severe mood swings. His servants hired a harpist, hoping the sweet music would soothe him. The harpist was a young shepherd named David, who became a favorite at the king's house. Later David became a big hero for killing the giant Goliath. Saul was so jealous of David's popularity that his depression returned. Saul plotted to kill David. His hostility led to a war in which he and his sons were killed, leaving David as the king of Israel.

In the fifth century BC, a Greek doctor named Hippocrates treated patients who had melancholia, a "humor," or mood disorder, that left people feeling "sleepless, irritable and restless." Centuries later, in the

1600s, Hamlet, the moody title character in William Shakespeare's play *Hamlet,* said these bleak words:

> *How weary, stale, flat and unprofitable*
> *Seem to me all the uses of this world.*

And although few people are aware of this, in the mid-nineteenth century U.S. President Abraham Lincoln was so troubled by depression that he wrote a letter to his girlfriend describing himself as "the most miserable man living."

Today, depression is just as painful and destructive. It affects people of all ages, nationalities, religions, and races. There are various types of depression. One of the most frequent and most complex is manic depression, known to professionals as bipolar disorder. Bipolar means that your moods swing back and forth between two opposite emotional states. The prefix "bi," which means two, refers to the two moods of bipolar disorder, and the ending "polar" refers to the opposite states or poles that characterize the illness.

This means that you experience periods of major depression in which you feel sad, lonely, weak, and helpless. Other times you have manic periods in which you feel incredibly energetic and confident and experience extreme sensations of anger, irritation or happiness. Your mood might go from low and despairing (during the depressed phase) to elated—extremely happy—and hypersensitive (during the manic phase) and then back to low and despairing again. Because these phases are so radically different and are often interspersed with seemingly "normal" periods, bipolar disorder is often difficult to diagnose. Take, for example, the case of Lucy.

*Lucy first began feeling strange after her thirteenth birthday. At times she heard a buzzing in her head that made her irritable. At home she snapped at her parents, whose comments she thought were stupid and boring. Meanwhile, school was slowly becoming intolerable. Teachers droned on and on and classes seemed never-ending. They were so tiresome she wanted to scream. Sometimes, Lucy felt as if she were screaming in her head.*

*By the time she entered high school, Lucy had stopped doing her homework and had begun cutting classes. For nights at a time, she could not sleep. Her behavior was very irregular. Once, during a sleepless night, she decided that she did not have any interesting clothes. She pulled all of her clothes out of her closet and threw them on the floor. The next day, she stole her mother's credit card and went on a crazy buying spree.*

*After the second time Lucy stole her mother's credit card, her mother threatened to kick her out of the house. By then, Lucy wasn't getting along with her parents at all. Any discussion led to a massive fight with Lucy screaming hysterically.*

*Even Lucy's friends thought she was acting weird. They stopped inviting her out with them. "What's with you?" they asked her. "How come you're acting so strange? You've been really irritable lately."*

*Lucy had been feeling increasingly annoyed with everybody. She didn't know what was wrong with her. She felt alone and did not know where to turn. Everybody seemed to be against her.*

*Lucy thought that she heard whispering behind her back. The whispers joined the buzzing in her head, and at times she felt as if she were going crazy. Nights were the worst. She was so nervous that she snuck out of the house and went for long walks. If she stayed at home, she would jump out of her skin. On her walks, Lucy discovered some after-hours bars that would serve minors. She would drink a few beers, hoping that this would help to relax her, but it didn't seem to work. She started drinking harder stuff, like tequila and gin.*

*Lucy was barely showing up at school. The school principal finally had a talk with her parents about how difficult she had become. The principal wondered if there was something wrong at home. Afterward, Lucy's parents were furious. "Why are you acting like this?" her mother demanded. Her dad yelled at her, "You're ruining your life!"*

*Lucy tried to turn over a new leaf. For a while, things seemed okay. She went back to school and tried to pay attention. At night, with her parents watching over her, she tried to do homework. Her friends still ignored her. Nobody understood. Everything was becoming too much of an effort. She was still drinking, only now it was not to relax but because she needed a pick-me-up.*

*Then Lucy crashed. One day, shortly after she started walking to school, Lucy turned around and went home. All she wanted to do was to stay in bed and cry. She had never felt so useless and miserable in all her life. When her parents saw her in this state, they realized that Lucy was not just a rebellious teenager acting up. They realized that she had a real problem and that she needed help.*

*Lucy's mother talked with the counselor at Lucy's school and with the family doctor. Both said it sounded as if Lucy were suffering from some kind of depression. They recommended that Lucy and her parents see a psychiatrist. Lucy did not want to see anybody. She had never felt so low. It seemed impossible that anyone would be able to help her or that she would ever feel better. Her parents pleaded with her. They finally got angry and yelled at her. Lucy didn't care. She felt as if she had plunged into the bottom of a well and couldn't climb out.*

# Chapter One | What Is Bipolar Disorder?

**L**ike adults, most teens go through periods when they feel sad or blue. At these times, you may slam the door to your room and feel like hiding your head under the pillows. Maybe you do not feel like talking to your parents or hanging out with your friends. You might be feeling angry or irritated. Maybe you think of yourself as a loser. Sometimes these feelings are reactions to a problem. Perhaps you are sick with a bad case of flu, you're having some trouble at school, or your best friend is mad at you. Within a week or two, you will probably start to feel a little better.

However, although feelings of depression come and go, the illness that is depression can stay around and often get worse. Depression is a disease, just like diabetes or bronchitis, that can get worse if left untreated by a professional. Depression affects your emotional state, leaving you exhausted or panicky, teary or desperate. It also affects your physical well-being. Depressed people often feel constantly tired. They may experience headaches and stomachaches or uncontrollable shaking and fidgeting.

According to the American Psychiatric Association (APA), one out of every five Americans will experience serious depression during his or her lifetime. Sadly, the APA estimates that the majority of depressed people fail to recognize the illness and get help. If they stop eating regularly and feel constantly worried, these people blame it on stress. If they can't think straight, it's because they don't get enough sleep. If they feel tired and achy, they think they must have some bug. In the meantime, the real problem—depression—stays unresolved and often gets worse.

## Teens and Depression

For a long time, it was thought that only adults could be victims of major depression. In fact, there are increasing numbers of teens that are affected by depression. According to the National Institute of Mental Health (NIMH), of the 18 million Americans who are depressed, up to an estimated 2 million are teenagers. Some mental health experts think that as many as 20 percent of high school students are very unhappy or suffer from a mood disorder. Teenage years are filled with change, so it is natural to experience a lot of ups and downs. You suddenly have new pressures to cope with as you try to

Depression can have physical conse-
quences, such as stomach pain.

come to terms with your changing attitudes toward your parents, friends, and teachers. Some of the new things you are dealing with will be confusing. Why do you feel furious when your best buddy starts spending a lot of time with his new girlfriend? Why does the size of your growing breasts make you so embarrassed that you start cutting school to get out of gym class?

It is important to let people whom you trust know how you are feeling and what you are going through. Adults sometimes make the mistake of seeing teens as naturally moody. They will say things like "You are in your terrible teens" or "You're just going through a difficult phase." This is why it is often hard to detect depression in teens and why real problems are easily ignored.

## Manic Depression

Generally, people with bipolar disorder do not swing evenly like a pendulum back and forth from manic to depressive states. More often than not, the cycles of mania and depression are unpredictable and can last for very different lengths of time. You can even experience both at the same time. Many people with bipolar disorder have extreme cycles only once every few years. Yet rapid cyclers go through four or more episodes of mania and depression each year. Ultrarapid cyclers have episodes within a week, and ultradian cyclers have distinct mood swings within just twenty-four hours.

At the same time, some manic-depressives may go for weeks, months, or even years without experiencing any extreme ups and downs. Instead, they have normal moods like everyone around them. Psychiatrists call this euthymia. A milder form of bipolar disorder is called hypomania. A hypomanic episode will leave you feeling suddenly energized, outgoing, extremely happy, and enthusiastic. Hypomanic phases are never so severe that they will seriously disrupt your life. However, even though they feel good, they are eventually followed by depression.

## Who Gets Bipolar Disorder?

Bipolar disorder is often a hereditary disease, meaning that it runs in the family. However, just because one of your relatives has it does not necessarily mean that you will get it too. Although young children can be diagnosed with manic depression, the illness more frequently appears in young adults and continues throughout life. Teenage guys and girls are equally likely to experience bipolar disorder, but it is often more apparent in girls. This is because girls tend to find it easier to talk about their feelings than guys do. Sometimes guys feel that admitting to being depressed means that they are weak and have no control. They tend to suppress or hold back their feelings. In the long run, this only makes life more painful and difficult.

# Chapter Two | Symptoms of Bipolar Disorder

**B**ipolar disorder is often difficult to diagnose. Frequently, when the illness first appears, both manic and depressive phases might be somewhat mild. Teens might feel irritated, anxious, or aggressive without knowing why. A real clue is if you start behaving hyperactively or as if you have too much energy.

Because these symptoms change and are not very obvious early on, both you and those around you—even your doctor—might blame something else for your moods and difficult behavior. According to statistics, two out of three times, doctors fail to recognize symptoms of bipolar disorder initially. Also, when manic-depressives are in a milder manic phase—full of happiness, energy, and confidence—they and those around them never stop to think that anything is wrong.

Bipolar disorder can be difficult to diagnose and treat.

# Depression vs. Being a "Typical" Teenager

Many of the symptoms of depression resemble the normal moods and feelings that adolescents experience. This is another reason why depression is hard to diagnose. As you grow and your body changes, the levels of hormones (chemicals in your brain and bloodstream) increase and sometimes set your body chemistry out of whack. These chemical imbalances can leave you feeling stressed out, sad, or extremely emotional. This is natural. For the most part, it is also usually temporary. However, if such feelings are very intense and keep lasting day after day, you might be depressed.

*Roberto had always had times when, for no apparent reason, he felt sad. As a little kid, his parents' friends made remarks such as, "Roberto's such a serious boy!"*

*When Roberto became an adolescent, his dad was always telling him to "lighten up," and his mother used to muss his hair in an irritating way and call him "Grumpy Face." Roberto did not know what was wrong. Then, in his second year of high school, he started having days when he didn't feel like getting out of bed. Roberto went to school and came home and went to school and came home, but he felt as if he were living under a dark cloud. Nothing meant anything. After weeks of feeling this way, he started wondering if this was just a phase. Maybe he was really depressed.*

Often teens realize that they are depressed before their parents or teachers suspect any problems. If you pay attention to your feelings, you can play a big role in taking care of yourself. Ask yourself the following questions: How extreme are the bad moods you have been experiencing? How long have you been having them, and how are they interfering with your day-to-day life? If they have been going on for more than a couple of weeks and are making it hard for you to function, you should definitely speak to an adult whom you trust and who can help you.

## Are You Depressed?

If you are concerned that you are depressed or that someone close to you is experiencing a form of depression, you may want to take a close look at the following questions. Do you or does someone you know seem to . . .

- ◆ Feel sad and anxious?

- ◆ Feel like a loser or feel responsible for things that go wrong?

- ◆ Get irritated by the slightest thing?

- ◆ Tend to overeat or perhaps feel unable to eat at all?

- Have no hope for the future?

- Have trouble enjoying things that used to be pleasurable?

- Feel weak or tired?

- Sleep too much or not enough?

- Explode with anger or have little self-control?

- Cut classes, skip meetings and activities, and avoid social events?

- Drink or take drugs, hoping to feel better?

- Find it difficult to concentrate or make decisions?

- Feel a lack of control?

- Have frequent headaches or stomachaches?

- Frequently think about or talk about death, suicide, or self-injury?

If the answer was yes to four or more of these questions and you have had these symptoms for more than two weeks, you might be seriously depressed. If you suspect that a friend or sibling is depressed, speak to a school counselor or an adult you can trust and let him or her know about your concerns.

## Mania

Mania is a state of high, unnatural excitement. If you are in a manic phase, you tend to become hyperactive,

Speak to a counselor or therapist about your concerns.

overflowing with nonstop energy. Often, having so much energy can leave you feeling worried or anxious. Mania can also lead to panic attacks, during which you become immobilized (unable to take action) because you fear anything and everything. During a panic attack, even a simple choice, such as deciding to turn on the television, can cause you anxiety. In extreme cases, you might experience hallucinations or hear voices.

> *One day, Janice was going home on the bus. There was a lot of traffic, and the bus seemed to be taking forever. Janice started getting nervous as more and more people got on. Then everything around her went foggy. She suddenly felt overcome by anxiety. Her heart was pounding, and she started sweating. The other passengers seemed to be closing in around her. The panic inside of her was so great that she started to cry.*

Sometimes a manic episode can make you obsessive. You may become overwhelmed with awful thoughts or desires. Other times, you might become compulsive and feel driven to do something—such as drink, smoke, or eat—by an inner force that seems stronger than your own will. This behavior can be dangerous, causing you to feel as if you have no control over yourself.

## Are You Manic?

Take a look at the list below and ask yourself these questions. Do you or does someone you know . . .

- Seem to need almost no sleep at all?
- Become easily distracted?
- Feel hyperalert and supersensitive?
- Fidget and move around nonstop?
- Act obnoxiously?
- Talk a lot and very quickly?
- Feel on top of the world?
- Become very irritable for no reason?
- Have trouble making decisions?
- Pull dangerous stunts and act invincible?
- Feel full of creative energy?
- Come up with lots of wild, impractical ideas?
- Drink and do drugs excessively?

If the answer was yes to four or more of these questions and you have been feeling these symptoms for more than two weeks, you might be experiencing a manic episode.

Although depression might appear to be the more serious of the two phases, the manic phase is usually more dangerous. When you are manic, you might stay awake for days or even weeks at a time. Although you feel as if you are bursting with energy, your nonstop activity will eventually drain your body's energy reserves, leaving you weak, exhausted, possibly even dehydrated. With your body's defenses down, you risk catching an infectious disease that a healthy body could normally have fought off.

At the same time, when you are experiencing a manic episode, your sense of judgment and reality goes out the window. This can lead to all sorts of excessive behavior, such as gambling and spending sprees, drinking and drug taking, and promiscuous sex and physical risk taking—speeding in a car, for example. The results of such activities—unplanned pregnancies, the risk of sexually transmitted diseases, maxed-out credit cards or a loss of funds, getting kicked out of school or fired from a job, troubles with the police, alienation from friends and family—can wreck a person's life.

# Chapter Three | What Causes Bipolar Disorder?

**S**cientists do not know exactly what causes bipolar disorder. However, most agree that the condition is due to certain chemical imbalances in the brain. This is why manic depression is considered a real physiological condition and not simply a psychological illness. Episodes of mania or depression can be brought on or aggravated by a combination of the following four major factors:

## Biochemical Factors

Studies show that some depressive disorders—bipolar disorder in particular—are caused by chemical imbalances in your brain. Your brain produces and uses chemicals called neurotransmitters, which send messages through your nerve cells to your entire body. People experiencing mania usually have too many

Some depressive disorders are caused by chemical imbalances.

neurotransmitters being produced, whereas people in a depressed cycle often have too few. Such excesses or deficiencies upset the communication between your brain and your body. Although much about neurotransmitters is still being researched by scientists, once an imbalance is detected, doctors are often able to readjust levels with the use of medicine.

# Genetic Factors

If there is a history of depression in your family, this can increase your chance of developing bipolar disorder. Scientists believe that there might be genes that can be inherited that make you more susceptible to manic depression. However, just because someone in your family has manic depression does not mean that you will acquire it. Also, many people with bipolar disorder come from families with no history of depression.

# Environmental Factors

Your environment is made up of the things you do, the people with whom you interact, and the spaces you inhabit on a daily basis. There will always be some aspects of your environment that you will have no control over. When this happens, it is easy to feel overwhelmed and anxious. It might be a bully at school who always picks on you, your parents who fight a lot, or the death of a close friend or relative. Peer pressure,

Coping with the death of a loved one can cause psychological problems.

financial troubles at home, sickness, and divorce are other events that can leave you feeling very unhappy.

When you are under pressure, your body tries to help you by producing increased amounts of certain hormones. Like neurotransmitters, hormones carry messages between your brain and your nerve cells. When you are anxious or afraid, you will often have excess amounts of a stress hormone called cortisol. Many depressed people often have higher than normal levels of cortisol. If these high levels stay in your body for a long time, they can have an effect on both your brain and your nerve cells. The changes that result can lead to serious depression.

## Psychological Factors

Regardless of biochemical and genetic factors, your attitude can affect the way that a depressive illness affects you. If you tend to look at things negatively, if you lack self-confidence, and if you worry too much and find it difficult to talk about problems, you will be less able to deal with the mood swings you are experiencing. You also have a stronger chance of becoming seriously depressed.

Teens who have had a difficult childhood might be more susceptible to depressive disorders. Tense family situations, major illnesses, troubles in school, and lots of moving around can make you feel insecure and uncertain about the future. It can make coping with manic depression very difficult.

# Chapter Four | Diagnosing Bipolar Disorder

**D**iagnosing manic depression is often more complicated than diagnosing major depression. This is because of the manic aspect of the illness. When you are manic, you often feel on top of the world. If you experience a strong manic episode—where you are talking nonstop, bouncing off the walls, feeling hypersensitive, and bursting with enthusiasm—you won't believe anything is wrong with you. If somebody tries to tell you that you are acting strangely or obnoxiously, chances are you will be feeling so high and mighty that you won't believe it.

## Difficulties in Diagnosing Teens

As was mentioned in chapter two, it is often more difficult to diagnose bipolar disorder in teenagers than in adults. One reason is that society is conditioned to think of teens as naturally moody, unpredictable, and difficult. Initially, symptoms of both mania and depression can be confused with normal teenage behavior. Another difficulty is linked to differences between depressed adult versus depressed teen patterns of behavior. Whereas it is common for adults to express their depression openly, many teens deal with depression by acting up. You might be rude and hostile, or you may feel reckless and do careless things. Some kids might not understand what they are going through, let alone know how to express it. Often, their excessive behavior is a cry for help.

*"When I was manic, I was so out of control," says Jezebel, sixteen. "I was obnoxious. I wouldn't shut up. For no reason at all, people annoyed me. I'd get angry and try to annoy them in return. I got expelled from school for being 'problematic.' Then I started stealing things. Of course, I got arrested. Soon after, I started seeing a psychiatrist. Working with her, I realized I wasn't an awful person. I had a real illness, and that was what was making me act this way."*

More often than not, parents or teachers punish troubled teens for being "bad" instead of taking a deeper look at the reasons behind the destructive behavior. If you are feeling strange, unhappy, or anxious, it is important that you talk to someone about your problems. If you do not feel comfortable talking to your parents, try opening up to another adult you trust:

a relative, a teacher or coach, a close friend's parents, a clergy member, a school guidance counselor, or a social worker. Once you are aware that you have a problem, you will have to see a doctor in order to identify what kind of depression you have.

Bipolar disorder is not like other diseases that you can identify by simply taking a blood test. The first thing a doctor will do is collect information about your symptoms. He or she will ask about your feelings and behavior and will gauge the frequency and intensity of the manic and depressive symptoms you are experiencing (see chapter two). To make an accurate diagnosis, your doctor will need to speak with you and your parents in order to compile a complete patient history. You will likely be asked questions about the following five topics:

- Development—Did you have an easy birth? Were you a healthy baby without any problems learning to walk, talk, and so forth?

- Physical health—Were you a healthy kid? Did you have any illnesses, accidents, surgery, or medical conditions?

- Psychological health—As a kid, were you relaxed or anxious, timid or extroverted? Did you act up?

- Education—Have you always done well in school or have you had difficulty? Do you have trouble paying attention in class?

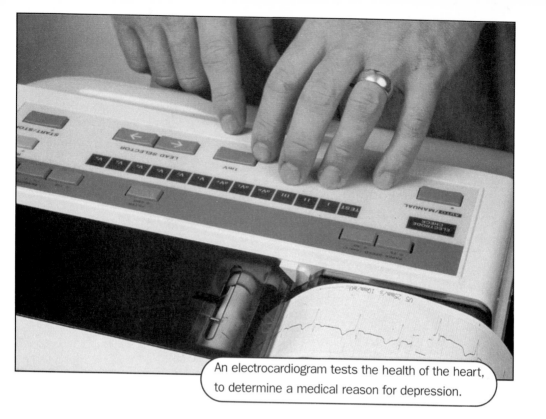

An electrocardiogram tests the health of the heart, to determine a medical reason for depression.

◆ Family—What are your relationships like with your parents and siblings? Are there any cases of mood disorders, learning disabilities, or alcoholism in your family?

You should have a normal physical examination as well as blood and urine tests and an electrocardiogram. This way a doctor can rule out any kind of medical reason for your symptoms of depression. Often psychological tests can help give doctors additional information about your state of mind. You might be shown pictures or images, such as the Rorschach inkblots, and be asked to give your interpretation of them. Often your impressions can give doctors insights into your fears and concerns.

# Chapter Five | Effects of Bipolar Disorder

**B**ipolar disorder can affect you in many different ways. It can cause you to experience certain sensations and to behave or act in various ways. Some of these sensations and reactions are common to all kinds of depressive disorders, but others are specific to manic depression. In particular, they are the results of the manic aspects of the disease.

## Creativity

Vincent Van Gogh, the Dutch painter, had five siblings; three had severe emotional problems, one of whom committed suicide. Van Gogh himself was a manic-depressive who experienced severe mood swings. When he sliced off his ear during a fit of despair, the painter Paul Gauguin, his extreme act was probably a result of

Vincent Van Gogh is believed to have suffered from manic depression.

his condition. When Van Gogh was depressed, he felt like an outcast and a failure. He began painting after he was unable to succeed at any other career. He created some of his finest work when he was in the midst of a manic episode. During one seventy-day period in France, he completed seventy paintings—one a day!

Like Van Gogh, many great artists found outlets for their extreme feelings and heightened perceptions through art. The novelists Mark Twain and Virginia Woolf, the poets Lord Byron and Edgar Allan Poe, the artist Michelangelo, the playwright Tennessee Williams, and the composer Robert Schumann all suffered from bipolar disorder. This is not just a coincidence. Scientists believe there is a link between creativity and manic depression. Recent studies indicate that during manic episodes, people tend to have a high creative output.

## Drug and Alcohol Abuse

Another common effect of bipolar disorder is resorting to the use of drugs and alcohol. Most often this is in order to dull the extreme moods experienced during both manic and depressive phases. Teenagers are particularly likely to turn to either or both substances for comfort. They are juggling confusing symptoms of bipolar disorder as well as peer pressure to drink and do drugs. However, these substances do not make you

Many sufferers of depression turn to drugs and alcohol.

better; all they do is temporarily mask your symptoms. Over time, they make your symptoms worse. Drugs and alcohol can act on your brain's neurotransmitters in a way that overstimulates the nerve cell pathways that govern your emotions. This can upset your natural mood-balancing systems, causing you to experience even more severe mood swings.

*"I started drinking and doing drugs because I didn't know who I was anymore," confesses Moss, seventeen. "My mood swings left me feeling as if I couldn't relate to anybody. I felt isolated. When I got high or wasted, it seemed like I could get along better with people. My friends thought I was out of control. So I drank more. It*

*was a vicious cycle. Then one time, I OD'd and ended up being hospitalized. Afterward, I went into a detox program. Now I'm on medication for manic depression, but I also go to Alcoholics Anonymous to help me stay clean."*

The National Institute of Mental Health (NIMH) has found that abuse of alcohol and cocaine is especially high among those with manic depression. This is not surprising if one considers that manic-depressives not only frequently have a family history of mood disorders but are also likely to have a family history of alcoholism. In fact, according to the NIMH, 60 percent of people who are found to have bipolar disorder are also diagnosed with drug or alcohol abuse.

What complicates matters is that the symptoms of bipolar disorder and substance abuse are so similar, particularly manic symptoms such as feelings of invincibility and irritability, the inability to make rational judgments, and extreme highs. As such, doctors often have a tough time diagnosing what your primary problem is: manic depression, alcoholism, or drug addiction. This can affect how doctors choose to treat you. They might work on curing your addiction before dealing with your mood swings, they might stabilize your mood swings before attacking your substance abuse, or they might treat both at the same time.

# Suicide

Teens who suffer from bipolar disorder are often at risk for suicidal behavior. A combination of many factors—depression, substance addiction, stress, an unhappy family situation, and difficulties with peers—can increase the risks of you thinking about, attempting, and committing suicide. Suicide is the third leading cause of death among youths between the ages of fifteen and twenty-four. Some studies show that close to 11 percent of high school students admit to having tried to kill themselves at least once. Statistically speaking, every day an average of eighteen teens commit suicide in the United States.

Severe depression in particular, with its accompanying feelings of overwhelming hopelessness and loneliness, can make teens especially vulnerable to suicide. In fact, people who suffer from bipolar disorder are thirty times more likely to commit suicide than those without a mood disorder. When coupled with substance abuse and aggressive behavior, the risks for suicide grow even higher. Sadly, between 20 to 50 percent of manic-depressives attempt suicide at least once.

It is tragic when depressed teens choose a permanent solution to solve a temporary problem. Killing yourself is a mistake you can't learn from, and the one sure thing about life is that things are always bound to change. Bipolar disorder can be treated, and most of those diagnosed with the illness, who find a suitable treatment, can and do live healthy, stable lives.

Often when you're alone with your problems, they seem a lot worse. That is why it is very important to make an effort to talk about your problems. Don't be afraid that people will think you are weak because you are depressed and need help. Talking about your problems and seeking help means taking responsibility for yourself. This shows a lot of strength. Knowing you are not alone and that people can and want to help you is one of the best protections against suicidal thoughts.

# Chapter Six | Treating Bipolar Disorder

**A**ccording to the National Institute of Mental Health (NIMH), less than 30 percent of people suffering from depression seek treatment. This is especially true of teens suffering from bipolar disorder. When you are going through a depressed episode, you will likely feel so tired and hopeless that getting help will seem impossible. By contrast, when you are in a manic phase, your sensations of extreme happiness, self-confidence, and invincibility will persuade you that you have never felt better. In between both mood extremes, you will likely have moments—even periods that last for months—when you feel normal.

*Eighteen-year-old Lydia experienced her first manic episode when she was fourteen. "I had no idea what was happening," she says. "I started acting hyper. I couldn't calm down. My parents said it was my hormones acting up and it would pass. And a few weeks later, it did, and I felt normal. A year later I started feeling depressed and tired all of the time. My parents still thought it was my hormones. It took three more years and more serious episodes to figure out that it was more than just hormonal imbalances."*

Take a good look at yourself. Think about what you have been feeling and how you have been acting. It might help to keep a journal where you write down exactly what thoughts are going through your head on any given day. Rereading the journal will allow you to judge your state of mind over time and to put your behavior into perspective. If what you read worries you, get help. There are some things you can't deal with yourself. Bipolar disorder is a serious illness, just like malaria or pneumonia. If you had either of these diseases, you definitely would not try to cure it yourself—you wouldn't know how. The same goes for manic depression. You need professional help.

Getting help works. If the bad news is that manic depression is a chronic illness for which there is no cure, the good news is that if carefully and consistently treated, most cases of bipolar disorder can be controlled, allowing you to function normally. It is essential, however, that you get a proper diagnosis as soon as you recognize your symptoms. Because different people experience bipolar disorder in varying ways, they also need to be treated in different ways.

When you are looking for a professional, make sure you find one who specializes in teen depression. As we saw in chapter four, teens often react to both depression and manic depression in ways that are quite different from adults, and manic depression in teens can be more difficult to diagnose. For this reason, you need to find someone who really understands depressed teens because he or she works with them on a regular basis.

## Who Can Help?

Many different professionals can get you help and can treat you themselves. Sometimes the variety can seem confusing. The following is a description of practitioners and their specialties:

- General physicians (such as your family doctor) can help to identify manic depression, following a physical examination and a discussion of your symptoms and feelings. They can then refer you to a specialist for help and treatment.

- Clinical social workers have advanced training in social work with an emphasis on emotional disorders. They can help you and give you information.

- Psychiatric nurse practitioners are nurses trained to deal with mental disorders. They can assess you, test you, diagnose your depression, and provide medication and therapy.

- Psychotherapists and counselors are trained to listen to you and help you deal with your feelings and symptoms.

- Clinical psychologists specialize in human behavior. They can assess you, test you, diagnose your depression, and provide therapy.

- Psychiatrists are medical doctors who specialize in mental health. They can assess you, test you, diagnose your depression, and provide medication and therapy.

In the case of bipolar disorder, the most effective treatment is a combination of carefully controlled and continued medication along with therapy and good lifestyle habits. A combination of all three is the best way to avoid hospitalization and suicidal behavior.

## Medication

The traditional medication used for bipolar disorder is a natural substance called lithium, which functions as a mood stabilizer. Because lithium in high doses can be toxic (in low doses it can be ineffective), you will need to monitor your medication very carefully by having regular blood tests to check the level in your system. Although lithium is generally very successful, it doesn't always work. Also, the side effects, which can include gastro-intestinal problems, weight gain, shaking, and fatigue, can sometimes be difficult to live with, even though several new drugs now exist to help diminish these problems.

In 1995, the Federal Drug Administration (FDA) approved another mood stabilizer called Depakote, which comes from a substance called valproic acid. Other medications that have not yet been FDA approved are also being used to treat manic depression. One of the most successful of these is Tegretol. These medications may be taken individually, in combination with lithium and/or each other, and together with other medications.

Your doctor might also prescribe antidepressants such as Zoloft, Paxil, or Prozac as well as mood stabilizers, especially if you have long and deep episodes of depression. However, using antidepressants without also using a mood-stabilizing drug may be dangerous because it might cause you to have a manic phase very quickly. Even if you are taking both an antidepressant and a mood stabilizer, you must be carefully monitored.

Treating manic depression is complex because what works for one person might not work for another. Sometimes a combination of medications is effective, including the use of antipsychotics, benzodiazepines, thyroid supplements, and sleeping aids. These varying mixtures are sometimes called med cocktails or meds. Although med cocktails can be successful, they can sometimes have hard-to-take side effects, and you might still experience the odd episode of mania or depression. Like many medications, they could take weeks or even a couple of months to take full effect.

Bipolar patients usually have to take medication in specific doses at specific times every day. What is really essential is that you always take your medication, even if you are feeling fine. Often, people in a manic phase will feel so good that they think they don't need any medicine, or their heads will be so filled with thoughts that they forget to take their medication. This can be dangerous because going off such strong drugs—or taking them at the wrong time or in the wrong quantities—can mess up your delicately balanced nervous system. Equally important is never to mix your medication with other drugs or alcohol.

Make a schedule and stick to it. Taking charge of your treatment will make you feel responsible and help you feel that you are controlling your disease instead of letting it controlling you. It is also a good idea to keep a journal or a mood chart to track how you are feeling. Share any changes with your doctor. You know better than anyone else does how the drugs are making you feel and what side effects they are giving you. Because medication works differently on everyone, and each individual can have his or her own specific variety of bipolar disorder, it is up to you to tell your doctor what is working and what is not.

## Therapy

Along with medication, it is essential to see a professional—usually a psychiatrist, a psychotherapist, or another mental health specialist—who is an expert on what you are going through and can help you sort out the complicated feelings and behavior that are a part of bipolar disorder. If you want to keep the disease under control, you will need help understanding it and learning the skills to cope with it. This is what psychotherapy is all about.

You can do psychotherapy individually, as a family, or in a group. Choose whatever you and your therapist feel works best for you. The important thing is to be in an atmosphere where you feel comfortable talking about your problems. Often it is useful to do some therapy with your family. Not only you but also those who live with you and are close to you need to learn how to live with, deal with, and treat this complicated illness.

When choosing a psychiatrist or therapist, it is essential that you get along with him or her. You should trust, respect, and feel comfortable with your therapist. If after three sessions, you feel that it is not going to work out, look for someone else. Don't give up on therapy altogether.

*Fifteen-year-old Bryant hated the idea of therapy. His feelings were confirmed after his first session with Dr. Passarot. "The guy was totally not my style," explains Bryant. "He just sat there and stared at me while I talked. He barely said anything at all.*

*"After that first session, I said I'd never go back to him or anyone else," says Bryant. "But my dad kept bugging me to give therapy another chance. So I contacted another doctor. Weirdly enough, Dr. Vakah and I hit it off right from the start. I was surprised. Now, I've been seeing him for six months. I even find myself looking forward to our sessions."*

Think of therapy as a private place, where you can work out your problems in a nonjudgmental space. Although nobody doing psychotherapy gets cured overnight (or even in a month), it can provide you with a vital outlet.

## Taking Care of Yourself

An important part of living with bipolar disorder is taking care of yourself. Although people around you, both professionals and friends and family, can help you, you are the one who knows best what you are going through. You are the one who can best take steps to make things easiest on yourself.

A healthy body goes hand in hand with a healthy mind.

A healthy body can have a really big impact on a healthy mind. Eat balanced, nutritious meals at least three times a day. Avoid alcohol, caffeine, and junk food with its excesses of sugar, salt, and artificial ingredients. All of these contain chemicals that will throw your body out of whack. It is a good idea to drink a lot of water, which has many health benefits and helps to prevent dehydration (sometimes a side effect of bipolar medications).

Exercise is also key. Among other benefits, it will help release stress and tension. Exercise gives you a jump start when you are feeling down and unable to move and provides you with a healthy outlet if you are suddenly flooded with manic energy. Choose a sport or activity that you enjoy and that is not too complicated to do. This way you can stick with it and make it a scheduled part of your life.

Stress can be part of anybody's life, but too much neglected tension can aggravate or set off episodes of mania or depression. Aside from medication and therapy, it is very important to learn to deal with stress yourself as much as you can. Part of this is learning how to relax. Relaxing is often more difficult than it would seem, and it takes some practice and concentration. Allow yourself plenty of downtime to kick back and watch a movie, ride a bike, or hang out with a good pal. Be good to yourself. Even if you feel weak and rotten sometimes, you are going through a lot and deserve some good times. Also make sure you sleep well. When you are weak and exhausted, both your physical and emotional defenses are down. If you are having problems sleeping, talk to your doctor, who can prescribe sleep medication.

Finally, although you can be your best caretaker, do not be afraid to share details of your condition with family and friends. Many people do not understand manic depression. They think "it's all in your head" or that "you're exaggerating." So explain it to them, and then don't be afraid to talk when you are feeling alone, desperate, or suicidal. Surround yourself with good people you can count on. Aside from friends and family, know that there are youth groups, specialized hotlines, and associations for people who suffer from depressive disorders, including bipolar disorder—all of which can help you.

*Thirteen-year-old Tara had been cooped up in her room for two weeks. She felt as if she were falling into a black hole and there was no way she'd ever make it out. She just wanted to feel nothing, instead of pain. So she found some of her mother's prescription sleeping pills and took a few. Actually, she took a lot.*

*When Tara woke up, she was in the intensive care unit of a hospital. She had just had her stomach pumped. Although she begged her parents, the nurses, and the doctors to let her go home, Tara ended up staying in the hospital for two weeks. Her parents said they just couldn't handle her at home, that they were afraid of what she might do. They said that she needed help and that being hospitalized, even against her will, was the only way.*

*While Tara was in the hospital, she underwent a lot of tests, both physical and psychological. She talked to doctors and a psychiatrist, who asked her all about her life. The psychiatrist explained that Tara was suffering from major depression. He prescribed some antidepressants for her. At first, Tara felt no difference, but then gradually she began to feel a little better. She left the hospital and returned home.*

*Tara planned to go to summer school and make up her lost semester. For about ten days she was really tired but felt increasingly calm. Then suddenly, she started to feel the old feelings of panic and irritability mounting in her. She was really scared. She didn't know what was happening to her, why the drugs were not working anymore.*

*Tara told her parents about her feelings, and together they went to consult another psychiatrist, Dr. Hradsky. After questioning her very closely about her symptoms, Dr. Hradsky said that she believed that Tara was suffering from bipolar disorder. She said that the doctors at the hospital had only detected the depressive phase of* the disease but that the antidepressants had triggered the beginnings of a manic episode. The psychiatrist prescribed a drug called lithium to stabilize Tara's moods.

"This is just a beginning," said Dr. Hradsky. "Both of us will have to monitor the effects of lithium on you. And we might have to change the dosage. Or try other drugs. You'll also have to come see me on a regular basis, both with and without your parents. It will take a while to learn exactly what treatments will work best for you, and for you to learn how to cope with being manic-depressive. But once we know what we're dealing with, if you are able to stay on top of things, chances are good that you'll be able to lead a normal, healthy life."

Now sixteen, Tara has come to terms with the fact that she is manic-depressive and will be so for the rest of her life. She keeps two books beside her bed. They are like bibles to her. In one book, she ticks off all the medicine she takes each day. It turns out that the lithium didn't work too well on her, so now she takes a combination of Tegretol and antidepressants. In the other book, she writes down the way she is feeling every day. If she starts noticing something strange, she immediately lets Dr. Hradsky know. She sees Dr. Hradsky twice a week for therapy. Sometimes she feels, why *bother? Other times she feels that nothing is really wrong with her at all. However, she has missed only a few appointments.*

*There are still days when Tara feels rotten. There are other days when she feels nervous and irritable. Although the feelings sometimes overwhelm her, at least she knows where they are coming from, as do her parents, her teachers, and her close friends. When she tried to explain the illness to them, some of her friends did not understand. They sort of drifted away from her. Others, however, have been supportive. When Tara gets down or a bit hyper, they know not to take it personally.*

*Tara is doing okay in school these days, although she still has extra credits to make up. Sometimes she has trouble concentrating. She joined the swim team and does yoga to relax. Dr. Hradsky put Tara in touch with a support group for teens with bipolar disorder. They meet once a week, and it is a great comfort to talk to kids her own age who experience the same things that she does. In the end, she knows her old friends care but they do not understand what it is like. These kids do, and that is reassuring.*

*It's not as if everything is perfect, and maybe it will never be. Still, it is so much better than it was before.*

# Glossary

**antidepressants**  Medication prescribed to alleviate depression. Three of the most common are Zoloft, Paxil, and Prozac.

**bipolar disorder**  Illness in which emotions swing between two (bi) opposite (polar) emotional states. The clinical term for manic depression.

**compulsiveness**  A psychological state of being strongly driven to do something.

**Depakote**  A mood stabilizer used to treat manic depression.

**downers**  Mind-altering drugs that give you a sensation of feeling calm and relaxed.

**electrocardiogram**  Shows the changes of electric potential that occur during a heartbeat.

**genetic**  Relating to genes; something that is hereditary.

**hormones**  Chemicals that carry messages between your brain and your nerve cells.

**hyperactivity**  A state of being excessively active, energetic, and unable to concentrate.

**hypomania**  A mild form of manic depression in which manic phases are less extreme.

**lithium**  A natural substance commonly prescribed as a mood stabilizer for manic depression.

**mania**  Psychological state in which you feel excessive energy, happiness, and enthusiasm.

**neurotransmitters**  Chemicals that your brain uses to send messages to the rest of your body.

**obsessiveness**  Psychological state in which you focus excessively on a single feeling or idea.

**physiological**  Relating to the workings of the physical body.

**psychological**  Relating to the workings of the mind.

**psychotherapy**  Treatment of mental or emotional disorders through psychological analysis.

**Rorschach Inkblot Test**  Psychological test in which you interpret abstract ink patterns.

**Tegretol**  Mood stabilizer used to treat manic depression.

**uppers**  Mind-altering drugs that give you the sensation of feeling high.

# Where to Go for Help

## In the United States

American Psychiatric Association
400 K Street NW
Suite 1101
Washington, DC 20005
(800) 368-5777
Web site:http://www.psych.org

Depression Awareness, Recognition, and Treatment (DART)
National Institute of Mental Health (NIMH)
5600 Fishers Lane
Rockville, MD 20857
(800) 421-4211
Web site: http://www.nimh.nih.gov

Lithium Information Center
Dean Foundation
8000 Excelsior Drive, Suite 208
Madison, WI 53717
(608) 836-8070
Web site: http://www.healthtechsys.com/mimlithium.html

National Alliance for the Mentally Ill
2101 Wilson Boulevard, Suite 302
Arlington, VA 22201
(800) 950-6264
Web site: http://www.nami.org

National Depressive and Manic-Depressive Association
    (NDMDA)
750 North Franklin Street, Suite 501
Chicago, IL 60610
(800) 826-3632
Web site: http://www.ndmda.org

National Foundation for Depressive Illness
P.O. Box 2257
New York, NY 10116
(800) 248-4344
Web site: http://www.depression.org

National Mental Health Association
1021 Prince Street
Alexandria, VA 22314
(800) 969-NMHA
Web site: http://www.nmha.org

## In Canada

Canadian Mental Health Association
CMHA Ontario Division
180 Dundas Street West, Suite 2301
Toronto, Ontario M5G 1Z8
(416) 977-5580
e-mail:division@ontario.cmha.ca
Web site: www.ontario.cmha.ca

The Centre for Addiction and Mental Health
33 Russell Street

Toronto, Ontario
M5S 251
(416)-595-6878
(800)-463-6273

The Clarke Institute of Psychiatry
250 College Street
Toronto, Ontario
M5T 1R8
(416) 595-6878
e-mail: foundation@camh.net
Web site: http://www.clarke-inst.on.ca/

The Mood Disorders Association of Ontario and Toronto
40 Orchard View Boulevard, Suite 222
Toronto, Ontario
M4R 1B8
(416) 486-8046
(888) 486 8046

## Web Sites

Depression.com
http://www.depression.com

The Internet Mental Health Web Sit
http://www.mentalhealth.com

Pendulum Resources
http://www.pendulum.org

The Society for Manic Depression
http://www.societymd.org

# For Further Reading

Berger, Diane, and Lisa Berger. *We Heard the Angels of Madness: A Family Guide to Coping with Manic Depression*. New York: William Morrow & Company, 1992.

Cobain, Bev. *When Nothing Matters Anymore: A Survival Guide for Depressed Teens*. Minneapolis, MN: Free Spirit, 1998.

Duke, Patty, and Gloria Hockman. *A Brilliant Madness: Living with Manic Depressive Illness*. New York: Bantam Books, 1993.

Eshom, Daniel B. *Lithium: What You Should Know*. New York: Rosen Publishing Group, 1998.

Gelman, Amy. *Coping with Depression*. New York: Rosen Publishing Group, 1998.

Jamison, Kay Redfield. *An Unquiet Mind: A Memoir of Moods and Madness*. New York: Alfred A. Knopf, 1995.

Nelson, Richard E., and Judith C. Galas. *The Power to Prevent Suicide: A Guide for Teens Helping Teens.* Minneapolis, MN: Free Spirit, 1994.

Silverstein, Alvin, Virginia Silverstein, and Laura Silverstein Nunn. *Depression.* Springfield, NJ: Enslow Publishing, 1997.

# Index

# Index

## About the Author

Michael Sommers is a freelance author who has a master's degree in history and civilization. He grew up in Canada but is presently living in Brazil. He has a younger sister named Annie and a cat named Jesse.

## Photo Credits

Cover photo by Les Mills; p. 13 by Kristen Artz; p.17 by Ethan Zindler; pp. 21, 28 by Thaddeus Harden; p. 37, 49 by.Brian Silak; pp. 2, 35, © Corbis; pp. 26, 33 © Custom Medical.

## Layout Design

Michael J. Caroleo

## DATE DUE

| 5-2 | | | |
|---|---|---|---|
| | | | |
| | | | |
| | | | |
| | | | |
| | | | |
| | | | |
| | | | |
| | | | |
| | | | |
| | | | |
| | | | |